PRESENTED TO:

_____

BY:

_____

DATE:

_____

101 SIMPLE SECRETS

TO KEEP YOUR
LOVE ALIVE

HONOR B BOOKS

Inspiration and Motivation for the Season of Life

An Imprint of Cook Communications Ministries • Colorado Springs, CO

08 07 06 05 04   10 9 8 7 6 5 4 3 2 1

101 Simple Secrets to Keep Your Love Alive
ISBN 1-56292-277-7
Copyright © 2004 by Bordon Books
An Imprint of Cook Communications Ministries
4050 Lee Vance View
Colorado Springs, Colorado 80918

Developed by Bordon Books

Compiled by Betsy Williams, Tulsa, Oklahoma, in conjunction with Bordon Books.

INTRODUCTION

While no one can presume to have the perfect prescription for your marriage, an outside boost can often offer a much-needed shot of fresh enthusiasm for you and your mate. This handy guide is filled with sage advice and a dose of humor to help you build a vital, growing marriage. Consider these *101 Simple Secrets to Keep Your Love Alive* as your invitation to revitalize your marriage. With the advice packed in these pages, you'll be inspired to nurture a more meaningful, healthy, and loving relationship.

1

KISS, HUG, AND SAY,
"I LOVE YOU!"

et him kiss me with the kisses
of his mouth.

SONG OF SOLOMON 1:2

The world beyond the walls of your home can be a less-than-loving place. In fact, it can be downright vicious at times. Both you and your mate may drag through the door after a hard day's work with ragged and worn-down spirits, feeling emotionally bruised and abused.

Your words can serve as a healing balm to the wounded spirit of your mate, and this soothing cure is sure to spread to you as well. Guard the daily ritual of a good-bye kiss as you head your separate ways each morning. Come together each evening with a warm embrace. Say sweet words of love every chance you get.

DON'T LEAVE YOUR AFFECTION
TO SPECULATION.

2

SAY, "I'M SORRY."

An apology is the Super Glue of life. It can repair just about anything.

Contrary to the memorable line from the movie *Love Story,* sometimes love *does* mean having to say you're sorry. A sincere apology is not a sign of weakness. On the contrary, acknowledgement that you are at fault will strengthen your marriage as well as your spouse's admiration for you.

Don't let pride and stubbornness stand in the way of sincerely apologizing when you are wrong. We all have need of absolution at times. When those times come, the strength of your marriage will rest on your willingness to make things right with six little words: "I was wrong. Please forgive me."

ADMITTING A WRONG AND APOLOGIZING FOR IT IS THE QUICKEST WAY TO COOL A HOT SITUATION.

3

PAUSE BEFORE RESPONDING TO AN ANGRY OR CRITICAL REMARK.

---

t is best to listen much,
speak little, and
not become angry.

JAMES 1:19 TLB

Never allow anger to control you. In no place is this more important than in your marriage. Practice self-control by pausing for ten seconds before you answer an angry or critical remark.

When you respond too quickly, you tend to overreact and fan the flames of conflict. A timely pause not only gives you a chance to speak calmly, rationally, and thoughtfully, but it also provides an opportunity for your mate to reconsider their words. It's difficult to maintain a loving home life if we allow anger to engage us in conflict. But it will do wonders for your relationship when you handle volatile situations with finesse.

INSTEAD OF SHARPENING YOUR CLAWS, GIVE YOURSELF A CHANCE TO PAUSE.

4

CHECK YOUR BLOOD PRESSURE.

Look to your health; and
if you have it,
praise God.

Keeping your blood pressure in check is a gift you can give your spouse. The tricky thing is that high blood pressure frequently is not detected by how you feel. Getting a professional assessment by your physician takes only a few minutes, but it is vital if you are to get an accurate reading.

Hypertension means that your heart is working harder than it should to pump blood through your body. It increases your risk of stroke, heart disease, and kidney failure; but exercise, diet, weight reduction, relaxation techniques, and possibly medication can help.

Even if you are not concerned on your own account, you owe it to your spouse to live as healthily as possible. Make an appointment with your doctor today.

DO WHAT YOU CAN TO PUT OFF "TILL DEATH DO YOU PART" AS LONG AS POSSIBLE.

5

LOVE EXTRAVAGANTLY.

To ease another's heartache is to forget one's own.

There's one sure way to kill love—measure it. Loving someone because you think it's the right thing to do, because it's "your turn," or simply for what you can get isn't love at all. It's manipulation.

Keeping records of any kind can be bothersome, but with love, it can be deadly—especially to a relationship. If it's true that the more love you give away, the more you have, do yourself a favor and love abundantly. And be sure to include those who aren't in a position to return it. Give in secret. Volunteer. Pamper your spouse or a friend without expectations of the favor being returned. These loving deeds will benefit not only you but also everyone around you.

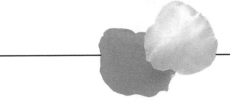

DON'T JUST LEND A HAND; GIVE YOUR HEART.

6

JUST SAY NO!

---

ust say a simple

yes or no.

JAMES 5:12 TLB

Does your mouth ever say yes while your heart is screaming no? Being assertive is sometimes viewed as being insensitive, unkind, or self-serving. But it's really just being honest and fair. Your time and your needs are as important as anyone else's.

This doesn't mean that your "boundaries" should keep you from ever going out of your way for someone else. It just means you don't let anger and frustration build by trying to live up to a yes that never should have been said in the first place.

Procrastination, forgetfulness, doing a halfhearted job, or backing out at the last minute are often just backhanded ways of saying no. So be considerate and just say no up front.

SAY NO, SO YOU CAN SAY YES TO THOSE THINGS THAT ARE MOST IMPORTANT TO YOU.

7

HOLD OUT YOUR HAND.

am always with you;
you hold me by
my right hand.

PSALM 73:23

Following the death of a spouse, many a bereaved widow or widower laments the fact that no one touches them anymore. Seldom—if ever—do people complain that their spouse touched them too much through the years.

Begin now to build a large reservoir of "touching" memories to cherish in your golden years. Extend your hand across the dinner table and give your mate's hand a gentle squeeze. Intertwine your fingers as you walk down the street. The simplest act of touching costs nothing, requires little effort, but pays big dividends if practiced faithfully. Your tender touch can convey love and a multitude of other positive emotions.

REACH OUT AND TOUCH
THE ONE YOU LOVE.

8

KEEP ONLY ONE CREDIT CARD.

A lways pay: for first or
last you must
pay your entire debt.

There are few things that can put stress on a marriage like debt and the management thereof. So why not avoid credit cards altogether? Unfortunately, it is now impossible to rent a car, travel without carrying a large amount of cash, or carry out a half dozen other functions we take for granted without at least one credit card.

So don't cut up all your credit cards—cut up all but one and use that one sparingly. Imagine your lives without the stress and anxiety of worrying about unpaid bills. Life will be much simpler and your marriage more peaceful.

DEBT AND WORRY ARE
SIAMESE TWINS.

9

TAKE A VACATION FROM TELEVISION.

The easiest way to find more time
to do all the things
you want to do is to turn
off the television.

Many people can't imagine living without television. Turning off the tube for good constitutes a drastic lifestyle change that few can manage cold turkey. Better results come when they wean themselves in smaller doses, starting with one day or even one evening. It also helps to plan a pleasant activity to enjoy together. Try reading a book together or engaging in a conversation on a topic of mutual interest.

Once you've broken the habit of automatically turning on the set, you will be able to practice the lost art of conversation. Time spent discussing the big things and the little things that are happening in your lives will bring a renewed intimacy to your relationship. The number of topics you can find to talk about may surprise you. You just may discover that your lives are every bit as interesting as those of your favorite sitcom characters.

TELEVISION IS A POOR SUBSTITUTE FOR REAL LIFE.

10

TREASURE YOUR TIME TOGETHER.

There is no more lovely, friendly, and charming relationship, communion, or company than a good marriage.

We often go to great lengths to protect our valuables. We polish our silver, wax the car, rent a safe-deposit box for the diamond jewelry we have inherited, and insure our possessions for the full replacement value. Yet we often neglect one of our most priceless treasures. A strong marriage demands an investment of time spent together—polishing and protecting, nurturing and affirming.

Don't underestimate the value of a good marriage. It can provide you with a lifetime of comfort, encouragement, and a strong sense of family even after the kids are grown and gone. Marriage, however, requires constant maintenance. Don't allow anything or anyone to interfere with those precious few moments you find to spend together.

INVESTING TIME IN
YOUR MARRIAGE YIELDS
PRICELESS RESULTS.

11

GO ON A WALK TOGETHER.

*y lover spoke and said to me,*
"Arise, my darling,
my beautiful one,
and come with me."

SONG OF SOLOMON 2:10

Go ahead! A stroll through the neighborhood will do both of you good in more ways than one. If you have children at home, saddle up the stroller or strap on their in-line skates. Walk just fast enough to get your heart pumping, but not so fast that you can't talk comfortably. Share the details of your busy day. Watch as the sun sets. Saunter in silence. Soak in the fresh air and the comforting sense of belonging to each other.

Convenient excuses *not* to walk abound, but you will quickly find that this new evening ritual is worth the effort. It will provide an opportunity to exercise your body and tone up your relationship. Don't put it off.

SPEND AT LEAST A FEW MINUTES OF EACH DAY WALKING OUTSIDE TOGETHER.

12

TWIST AND SHOUT!

When you finally allow yourself to
trust joy and embrace it,
you will find you dance
with everything.

Kids dance to any music that moves them, unlike adults who often have to be dragged onto a dance floor. Adults can be so self-conscious about how they look that they forget how great dancing feels. Dancing feels good for a reason. It stimulates endorphins, your body's natural mood-lifting hormones. It's also great exercise that has the added benefit of helping you express your feelings. That's a great combination, and the best thing is that you two can do it together!

So why be a wallflower? Take a dance class or just turn up the stereo and move to the beat. Who knew that having so much fun could actually be good for you!

THERE'S GREAT BENEFIT IN
A LITTLE BOOGIE-WOOGIE.

13

FORGIVE OTHERS.

e gentle and ready to forgive;
never hold grudges.
Remember, the Lord forgave you,
so you must forgive others.

COLOSSIANS 3:13 TLB

People hurt other people—intentionally or not, it's a fact of life. Holding on to that hurt forces you to carry a load that your body, particularly your heart, was not designed to handle. It robs you of energy that could be used for more positive things—like nurturing your marriage.

Forgiveness is a gift—no strings attached, regardless of whether the offender is repentant or has no remorse. It doesn't mean validating the action or excusing the wrongdoer. It means fully understanding how much you were hurt and choosing to release the offending person in spite of it. It's something you can do fully only through God, because He has done it so freely for you.

FORGIVING OTHERS IS A GIFT YOU GIVE YOURSELF.

14

READ A BOOK WITH YOUR MATE.

The pleasure of all reading is doubled when one lives with another who shares the same books.

Put aside the daily paper filled with depressing news. Instead, go to the nearest library or bookstore on an exploratory mission with your spouse. Search until you find a book that both of you would enjoy. Reclaim the long-forgotten pleasure of reading for enjoyment's sake. You'll find almost endless possibilities as you peruse the books on the shelves—how-to manuals, mysteries, biographies, or classics. Perhaps your mate would enjoy listening to your favorite childhood tale.

The fresh insight, information, and inspiration the two of you can glean from just a few minutes of daily reading will expand your base of shared experiences and provide new topics of conversation as well.

ENRICH YOUR MIND.
READ A BOOK.

15

DEAL WITH YOUR
EMOTIONAL BAGGAGE.

*The first rule is to keep an untroubled spirit.
The second is to look things
in the face and know them
for what they are.*

All human beings have painful experiences that have an impact on them at some level. They can affect the way we make decisions and relate to others, including our mates. If you experience feelings of guilt, failure, anger, or shame as a result of past experiences, don't ignore them. They are likely to intensify and will undoubtedly affect your marriage.

It will take some courage, but if you want to be a more secure, loving person and spouse, it's vital that you work to heal broken places in your heart. Take a look at yourself honestly. Be willing to talk with God, your close friends, your mate, or maybe even a professional counselor. The healthier you are emotionally, the healthier your marriage will be.

LIGHTEN YOUR LOAD—DROP YOUR EMOTIONAL BAGGAGE.

16

TALK, LISTEN, TALK, LISTEN, TALK, LISTEN . . .

When you talk you are only repeating what you already know— but if you listen you may learn something.

What a boost to your self-esteem to know that the one person in this world you value most is truly interested in your thoughts, opinions, and feelings. The give-and-take of communication is the nourishment that causes a marriage to thrive and grow.

Never assume that you know what your spouse is thinking or feeling. Care enough to devote your undivided attention. Hear what is being said. Don't simply nod as you mentally formulate your next response. Few compliments surpass the tribute of your genuine interest. For even better results, try putting your spouse first. Reverse the order of this bit of advice to listen, talk, listen, talk, listen, talk. . . .

PAY YOUR SPOUSE A TREMENDOUS COMPLIMENT— PAY ATTENTION!

17

DEVELOP A SENSE OF HUMOR.

Among those whom I like or admire, I can find no common denominator, but among those whom I love, I can: all of them make me laugh.

A good sense of humor is an immeasurable source of joy when shared with your mate. Tossing around comedic insights about this crazy life can foster a lighthearted atmosphere that will bring energy into your marriage.

If a good sense of humor does not come naturally to you, there are ways to cultivate one. Train yourself to be observant during conversations. You may find that something someone says triggers a funny memory or a play on words. Observe people who have a good sense of humor and note how they interject humor into everyday life and conversation. The important thing is to make an honored place for shared laughter with your spouse.

LAUGH YOUR WAY TO
A HAPPY MARRIAGE.

18

PRAY WITH YOUR SPOUSE.

Where two or three are gathered
together in my name,
there am I in the midst them.

MATTHEW 18:20 KJV

Never do two souls intertwine so closely as when they bow together in prayer. Inhibitions are set aside and a hallowed and holy tenderness transpires between a husband and wife who mutually recognize their need for and dependence upon God's intervention and blessing in their lives and marriage.

Today, take your spouse's hands in yours and offer a prayer to God. Begin by thanking God for your many blessings. Jointly present your burdens, cares, and concerns to God. Ask for His wisdom to meet the challenges of the day. Solicit His help. Invite the Almighty into your lives.

CEMENT YOUR MARRIAGE
WITH THE BOND OF PRAYER.

19

TAKE CARE OF YOUR OWN HEALTH.

Health is not valued until sickness comes.

If no one bothered to check and change the oil in the family car, the engine wouldn't last very long. Proper care and attention are also required in order for your body to function properly. Neglect may go unnoticed for a while, but eventually poor maintenance will catch up with you.

Few of us take care of our bodies with the same diligence that we give to our automobiles. We are either running on empty—skipping meals while racing through a stressful day, or we are filling up with bad fuel—those empty, sugar-filled calories. Stop long enough to schedule some routine maintenance. Fill your body with "high octane" foods. Slow down to a reasonable speed. It's difficult to invest in your marriage if you are sick or constantly exhausted.

HONOR YOUR BODY
BY GIVING IT THE
CARE IT NEEDS.

20

FIND A HOBBY YOU CAN SHARE.

*eople who cannot find time for
recreation are obliged sooner
or later to find time for illness.*

How long has it been since you have found a fresh new interest to share with your spouse? Rather than devoting precious leisure time to separate hobbies, look for activities that you and your mate both enjoy. Pursuing mutual hobbies and interests will divert your attention away from the stressful, hectic routines of everyday life and give you a chance to relax together.

Motorcycling. Golfing. Bird watching. Gardening. Stamp collecting. Fishing. Skydiving. Boating. There is a hobby tailor-made to fit every couple's budget, schedule, and energy level. You may simply need to experiment with several before you find the perfect hobby for the two of you.

HAVE THE TIME OF YOUR LIFE WITH THE LOVE OF YOUR LIFE.

21

REFUSE TO SPEAK NEGATIVELY ABOUT YOUR SPOUSE TO OTHERS.

A word rashly spoken cannot be brought back by a chariot and four horses.

A public forum is not the appropriate place to nurse a grudge. Even if you feel your spouse deserves your criticism, never air your anger and resentment in the company of others. Such an action often backfires.

As the afternoon TV talk shows have proven, an audience is more likely to inflame rather than quell an already volatile situation. When you criticize your mate publicly, you not only lower the listener's estimation of your mate, you lower their opinion of you as well. Stop before you speak those negative words. Ask yourself, *What do I hope to gain by criticizing my spouse to others?* You'll find that question rarely has a worthy answer.

DISAGREEMENTS SHOULD BE DISCUSSED BEHIND CLOSED DOORS.

22

NEVER GO TO BED ANGRY.

"In your anger do not sin":
Do not let the sun go down
while you are still angry, and
do not give the devil a foothold.

EPHESIANS 4:26-27

Like mushrooms growing in a dark and damp forest, anger sprouts into full-blown contempt during the night. Something about those long, dark hours seems to breed malice. Each tick of the clock intensifies a nighttime rage. Anger is a natural human emotion, but left to fester, it can do real damage to a relationship.

Don't take your anger to bed with you. Don't allow bitterness to fester until it does lasting harm. Expose your anger to the light as soon as it sprouts. Talk openly with your mate about the issue in question. Then forgive and do it quickly. Otherwise, it will be even more difficult in the morning.

PUT ANGER TO REST
BEFORE YOU RETIRE
FOR THE NIGHT.

23

BLOCK OUT TIME ON YOUR CALENDAR FOR A DATE WITH YOUR MATE.

he unfortunate thing about this world is that good habits are so much easier to give up than bad ones.

Before you enter any other appointments on your weekly planner, reserve a standing date night with your mate. Schedule this time as you would any important business meeting. Free nights seldom, if ever, magically appear. If your calendar or bank account won't allow for a weekly date, aim for a monthly rendezvous.

If you find it next to impossible to pencil in a Friday night movie date, consider a Saturday morning breakfast date at your favorite restaurant or a Sunday afternoon stroll through the park, Once you've mutually decided on the most convenient date, time, and place, religiously guard this important tryst. Don't let anything or anyone squeeze into this time.

CONTINUING TO DATE AFTER MARRIAGE HELPS KEEP THE ROMANCE ALIVE.

24

HIRE A MAID OR LOWER
YOUR STANDARDS.

---

*Where there is room in the heart
there is always room
in the house.*

If you're like most, living life gets messy, especially if you add children, pets, appliances that break down, and an occasional bout with the flu. Keeping a house that looks magazine perfect is a full-time job and doesn't allow much time for real living.

The flip side is that utter chaos can prove stressful and steal precious time from you. So what chores have to be done? Clean clothes, washed dishes, and groceries devoid of mold are all important. But dusting your baseboards? Family delegation and an occasional all-out spring cleaning, mixed with simply putting things away after you use them, is enough to keep most houses up and running, as well as more relaxed and inviting.

OWN YOUR HOME, BUT DON'T LET YOUR HOME OWN YOU.

25

EAT DINNER TOGETHER
AT THE TABLE.

When you have eaten your fill,
bless the LORD your God
for the good land he has given you.

DEUTERONOMY 8:10 TLB

Are you always eating on the run? Tonight, will dinner amount to grabbing a quick burger from a drive-thru? If so, you're missing out on an opportunity to communicate with your mate.

As often as possible, share your meal at the table in the quiet of your own home. Don't plan a big production, or your sit-down dinner plans will seldom materialize. The good china lends a nice touch but isn't necessary. Turn off the phone and let the answering machine pick up your calls. Listen to soothing music rather than the blaring television. Light candles to add a bit of romance to the room if you like. Provide a relaxing atmosphere for your evening meal, and watch it become nourishment for your marriage as well as your body.

IF YOU'RE TOO BUSY TO SIT AND EAT, YOU'RE TOO BUSY.

26

AGREE TO DISAGREE.

We all live under the same sky,
but we don't all have
the same horizon.

Few issues are worth a long-running feud or a heated debate with your mate. It's best to simply accept that you will not see things from your spouse's point of view at times and vice versa. Perhaps your differences of opinion center around a political viewpoint or a philosophical stance. Even the most perfectly matched couple should not expect to see eye-to-eye on everything.

When a disagreement surfaces, ask yourself, *Is this matter one in which we will ever be able to agree? Could this disagreement have a significant impact on our marriage? Is it worth the conflict that our relationship would have to endure?* Some battles are worth fighting. Others are not. Pick your battles carefully.

DON'T MAKE MOUNTAINS
OUT OF MOLEHILLS.

27

HEAD TO BED WITH YOUR SPOUSE.

---

ed is a bundle of paradoxes:
We go to it with
reluctance, yet we
quit it with regret.

Can you recall those sweet days of childhood when your parents lovingly tucked the covers under your chin and kissed you good night? Although you're all grown up now, those treasured, end-of-the-day warm fuzzies need not end. Institute a nightly ritual with your mate.

Don't leave your spouse dozing on the sofa as you tiptoe off to bed. Choose to go to bed together. Save at least enough energy to kiss each other and whisper "good night" on those evenings when you are both too tired for a romantic interlude. Dozing off together will increase your feelings of well-being and give you a head start on a good night's rest.

BEDTIME RITUALS AREN'T JUST FOR CHILDREN.

28

AVOID THE APPEARANCE OF EVIL.

Abstain from all appearance of evil.

1 THESSALONIANS 5:22 KJV

A lunch date with a coworker of the opposite sex may be strictly business. The late-night work session that includes the two of you may be legitimate. Nevertheless, if your actions cause others to raise a suspicious eyebrow, beware. Steer clear of any circumstance that might create even a twinge of jealously in your mate.

We live in a time when these precautions may be ridiculed by some as straitlaced nonsense. But keeping your actions above reproach guards against temptation and misunderstanding. It allows your spouse to rest more securely in the constancy of your love and faithfulness. No business matter is more important than your marriage.

TRUST NEVER FAILS WHEN INTEGRITY PREVAILS.

29

TREAT YOURSELF TO A MASSAGE.

He who refreshes others will himself be refreshed.

PROVERBS 11:25

A massage not only feels good, it's good for you. The motions used in massage trigger a natural relaxation response in your body, which slows down the nervous system. It also increases circulation, which helps relieve pain associated with excess tension. It reduces stress hormones, and increases seratonin, which provides feelings of well-being and enhances mental skills.

So why not make an appointment with a licensed massage therapist? If you're married, don't hesitate to treat your spouse. Research has shown that massage not only benefits the receiver but also the giver. Your husband or wife will undoubtedly want to return the favor.

MASSAGE IS GOOD FOR
THE BODY AND SOUL.

30

MAKE TIME FOR THOSE YOU LOVE.

---

*Wishing to be friends is quick work,
but friendship is
a slow-ripening fruit.*

Your marriage is your most important relationship, but strong relationships outside your marriage are important as well. Did you know that they can help protect you from colds and the flu? When your body is stressed, hormones such as adrenaline and cortisol are increased, which can lower your immunity to the "bugs" sharing your environment. But spending time with someone you care about and who you know cares about you could help to counteract some of these physical changes.

So pick up the phone. Make a date. Take time out from your crazy schedule just to be yourself with someone you love. Plan ahead or be spontaneous. Just don't put it off. Your body will thank you and so will your heart.

FRIENDS AND LOVED ONES
ARE GIFTS WORTHY OF
YOUR INVESTMENT OF TIME.

31

ASK GOD TO PROTECT AND
DIRECT YOUR SPOUSE.

---

*H*eaven is full of answers to prayers
which no one ever
bothered to ask.

How often do you think about your spouse in the course of a day? Each time your thoughts turn to your mate, institute a new habit—pause long enough to breathe a prayer on their behalf.

Do you know of specific problems or issues your spouse is facing? Take a moment to petition God for a special impartation of wisdom and guidance. Pray for special protection from any harm. Ask God to bless your mate with joy and peace in spite of life's difficulties. Before you say "Amen," thank God for allowing you to share your life with such a special person. Open your heart to supernatural insight into how you might increase your love.

PRAYER BRINGS YOU CLOSE
EVEN WHEN YOU'RE APART.

32

TELL YOUR SPOUSE WHAT YOU NEED.

Understanding human needs is half the job of meeting them.

As the years go by, it's easy to grow lazy in verbal communication, thinking that your mate automatically knows how you feel. It is an unfortunate characteristic of many long-term relationships. Couples engaged in great marriages have learned to overcome it.

Regardless of how good at mind reading your spouse may seem at times, only you can really know what's going on inside your head! Leave nothing to speculation or assumption, no matter how in tune with your thoughts your mate may seem to be. Put your thoughts into words. Assuming that another person—no matter how close—understands all of your needs, wants, and desires is foolhardy at best. Talk things over. Communicate.

A LACK OF COMMUNICATION LEADS TO UNMET EXPECTATIONS.

33

CHOOSE YOUR SPOUSE
AS YOUR BEST FRIEND.

For this reason a man will leave his father and mother and be united to his wife, and they will become one flesh.

GENESIS 2:24

An advice column in a popular women's magazine recently published an unusual inquiry. A bride-to-be wanted to ask her best friend, a man, to be her "maid" of honor in her upcoming wedding. She wanted to know the proper term for a man serving in this capacity. A better question for this woman might have been, *What hope does my marriage have for survival if the man I marry is not my best friend?*

Your marriage should encapsulate the ultimate of every earthly relationship. Your mate should be your best friend, your most trusted confidant, the first—and final—person you turn to when you need advice, comfort, and love. Is your spouse your best friend? If not, start working on that today.

FRIENDSHIP IS THE FOUNDATION OF EVERY GREAT MARRIAGE.

34

KEEP A POSITIVE OUTLOOK ON LIFE.

Attitudes are capable of making the same experience either pleasant or painful.

A single complaint often leads your thoughts down a depressing spiral of negativity. Negativity breeds faster than rabbits. Rarely does a complaining attitude produce positive results.

No matter how well things are going, most of us can find something to complain about. It is so easy to fall into the habit of negative thinking. Determine today to put an end to sour negativity and instead look for ways to improve your attitude. Commit a random act of kindness. Focus your attention away from your problems and onto the needs of others. Bless your spouse and those around you with a cheerful disposition.

A POSITIVE ATTITUDE ENGENDERS A POSITIVE RESPONSE.

35

ATTEND CHURCH WITH
YOUR SPOUSE.

---

et us not neglect our church meetings, as

some people do, but encourage and warn

each other, especially now that the day

of his coming back again is drawing near.

HEBREWS 10:25 TLB

By joining with like-minded believers in corporate worship, not only will your soul gain nourishment, your marriage will be strengthened as well. Here are just a few of the benefits church attendance offers a couple after they say, "I do."

Attending Church:

- Provides spiritual instruction and guidance.
- Turns your thoughts to the truths of Scripture.
- Brings to light areas of your life that may be contrary to Christian teaching.
- Develops your spirit's sensitivities and ability to love.
- Provides outlets for ministry and involvement in other people's lives.
- Focuses your attention on the majesty of God through worship and prayer.
- Empowers you and your mate through the development of personal faith in God.

SHARE A SPIRITUAL MEAL— GO TO CHURCH.

36

BRAG ABOUT YOUR SPOUSE
TO FAMILY AND FRIENDS.

---

*I can live for two months on
a good compliment.*

Your parents may feel that your mate doesn't quite live up to the high expectations they held for you. Your friends may view the one you married as an intruder. But when you consistently highlight the positive attributes of the love of your life, your praise should eventually wear down even the most stubborn skeptic.

Seize every opportunity to point out the many wonderful qualities you see in your mate. When you go overboard with genuine praise, the rewards are twofold: you reinforce for yourself how fortunate you are to be married to such a fantastic person, and you let others know you are not willing to entertain any criticism of your spouse.

FOCUS NOT ON THE WARTS
BUT ON THE WONDERS
OF YOUR MATE.

37

PUT YOUR SPOUSE
BEFORE YOUR WORK.

here's an opportune time to do things,

a right time for everything

on the earth.

ECCLESIASTES 3:1 MSG

Do you constantly work late? Do you put in long hours of overtime and drag yourself home each night exhausted? When you go out for dinner with your spouse, are your thoughts on the office rather than on the conversation? In subtle and not-so-subtle ways, your job may usurp your mate's rightful place in your priorities. The balancing act between vocation and family often proves tough to manage.

Your career may serve as more than just a means of earning an income. If so, that's wonderful. But when your job takes precedence over your family, it's time to reexamine your priorities. Both husbands and wives should view marriage as their first career.

MARRIAGE IS THE MOST IMPORTANT JOB YOU'LL EVER HOLD.

38

STROLL THROUGH THE MALL
ARM IN ARM WITH YOUR SPOUSE.

---

*Imparadis'd in one
another's arms.*

As divorce and discord prevail in many American homes, perhaps the time has come for happily married couples to exhibit a little PDA (Public Display of Affection). Rarely do we see spouses express genuine love and wholesome affection in public. Our world needs a few sweet reminders that true love within marriage can—and still does—last a lifetime.

Take pride in the fact that you are beating the odds. Use appropriate expressions of tenderness toward your mate wherever you go. Don't be surprised if you hear a few "ahhhs" by those who see you.

WHAT THE WORLD NEEDS NOW IS LOVE, SWEET LOVE.

39

EXPRESS YOUR INNERMOST
FEARS TO YOUR SPOUSE.

---

he only thing we have to fear
is fear itself.

Whatever anxiety you harbor—whether wildly irrational or distinctly possible—your first step is to bring it into the light. Trust your spouse enough to share your most secret worry. Through the simple act of admitting your innermost anxiety, you begin to break the stranglehold it has on you.

Let your spouse comfort you and tell you everything will be all right. Join your hands and hearts in prayer about your fear, and trust God to help you in your time of need. It's quite possible that this action will encourage your spouse to share their own fears. It will bring you closer together and provide a wellspring of comfort and affirmation as you attempt to overcome your fears and walk in faith.

TO OVERCOME FEAR,
YOU MUST EXPOSE IT.

40

AVOID VERBAL SPARRING, ESPECIALLY IN PUBLIC.

meal of bread and water in contented peace is better than a banquet spiced with quarrels.

PROVERBS 17:1 MSG

Even if you and your spouse fuss in apparent lighthearted fun, save the feuding for behind closed doors. When you constantly pick at one another in public, those observing you may begin to wonder how you treat each other when no one else is around.

Another faux pas is contradicting your spouse in public. When you do this in front of others, your audience begins to doubt your spouse's credibility. And your contradictory comments might be viewed as disloyal. As your spouse recounts a shared experience to others, bite your tongue if you are tempted to share that you remember it differently. Wait until the two of you are alone. And even then, instead of sparring, let kindness rule your discussion.

SAVE DISAGREEMENTS
AND CONTRADICTIONS
UNTIL YOU GET HOME.

41

PLAY AN ACTIVE ROLE
IN MONITORING YOUR
SPOUSE'S HEALTH.

All wealth is founded on health. To squander money is foolish; to squander health is murder in the second degree.

Teaching your mate new health habits can be difficult. For some reason, many people resist that type of interaction with their mate. However, it's too important to simply ignore. Consider buying a family health-club membership as a Christmas gift this year. Gently remind your spouse when it's time for a checkup, and be willing to go along for moral support, if necessary.

If your mate could stand to shed a few pounds, suggest that you diet together. At the very least, don't eat ice cream and cake when your spouse is around. By resisting the urge to nag or bully, you can do a lot to encourage your spouse to eat better, get plenty of sleep, and exercise.

DON'T LET POOR HEALTH ROB YOU OF YOUR GOLDEN YEARS TOGETHER.

42

RESIST THE URGE TO BE A FIXER.

---

*It is an honour for a man
to cease from strife:
but every fool will be meddling.*

PROVERBS 20:3 KJV

In our instant-everything society, it's easy to want to fix our spouse's problems immediately in order to ease their anxiety. It's a temptation to try to come up with a one-step, quick fix.

Often what our mates need the most is not a pat answer but a shoulder to lean on. Remind yourself that you are an invaluable help by simply listening. Many times people have the right answers locked inside of them. They just need some time to talk to someone attentive, someone who cares. All it may take is someone to ask intuitive questions in order to achieve the needed clarity.

HOUSEHOLD APPLIANCES NEED REPAIRMEN— YOUR SPOUSE DOES NOT.

43

PLAN A ROMANTIC GETAWAY.

You will never find time for anything.
If you want time,
you must make it.

A woman gave her husband a note he was to read as he left the office one day. He was to open the glove box of his car and read these instructions: "Pull out of your office parking lot and go three miles south. Turn left. Go 4.3 miles. Turn right . . ." and so on. Her husband was delighted when he arrived at the mystery destination. The directions led him to a hotel where his wife had planned a romantic getaway.

If you wait for a convenient time to break away with your mate, that time may never come. Why not arrange your schedule to include a mini-retreat this month?

ROMANCE IS THE FLAME THAT KEEPS MARRIAGE EXCITING.

44

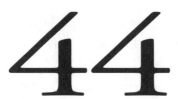

COMPLIMENT YOUR SPOUSE OFTEN.

To say a compliment well is a high art,
and few possess it.

Don't hold back. Let your mate hear complimentary words from your lips every day. Rather than criticism, use your words to praise and build confidence. Point out the physical attributes you find attractive. In addition, continually remind your spouse of the many reasons you are sure you married the right person.

Toss aside any misgivings you might have about building up your spouse too much. The world outside your door can be a belittling and demoralizing place. Make your home a refuge from society's steady rips. Let your spouse know that your eyes see the wonderful things that the world may never notice.

DECLARE YOURSELF AS YOUR SPOUSE'S NUMBER-ONE FAN.

45

DO NOT EXPECT YOUR SPOUSE
TO MEET ALL YOUR NEEDS.

y God shall supply all your need
according to his riches
in glory by Christ Jesus.

PHILIPPIANS 4:19 KJV

A good marriage demands reliance upon one another and a mutual effort to satisfy one another's needs. However, even the most devoted couples aren't capable of meeting each other's needs completely.

Surround yourself with a safety net of relationships—close friends and extended family—in order to stay emotionally healthy. Making your spouse exclusively responsible for meeting every emotional, physical, and spiritual need can damage even the most promising relationship. Acquire at least a basic knowledge of how to survive should your spouse be gone for an extended period. And remember to rely primarily upon God—not any human being—to satisfy the deepest yearnings of your soul.

NO ONE BUT GOD CAN MEET ALL YOUR NEEDS, BUT HE DOES IT WELL.

46

OFFER TO ATTEND AN ACTIVITY
YOUR SPOUSE ENJOYS.

Each of you should look not only
to your own interests, but
also to the interests of others.

PHILIPPIANS 2:4

If you really want to invest in your marriage, offer to join your spouse on an outing of their choice—and go cheerfully. Make no demands. Accept no reciprocal agreement. Whether this means whooping it up at a ball game or spending a few hours at a craft mall, this should be a "no strings attached" exercise done simply for love.

Don't stand in the shadows tapping your foot and impatiently glancing at your watch. Join in and make an effort to understand what your spouse enjoys about the activity. Purchase a special treat to celebrate the day. You may discover as you head for home that you enjoyed the day just as much as your spouse did.

NO TIME IS WASTED
WHEN IT'S SPENT MAKING
ANOTHER PERSON HAPPY.

47

REMEMBER THAT YOUR MARRIAGE IS YOUR MOST IMPORTANT RELATIONSHIP.

Grow old along with me! The best is yet to be,
The last of life, for which the first was made.
Our times are in his hand.

Parents often succumb to the temptation to pour all of their energies and attention into their children. Then when the day comes that the kids are gone, Mom and Dad can only stare at each other blankly, with nothing left in common.

Take care that the parent-child relationship does not supersede your relationship with your spouse. Keep alive mutual interests apart from your children. Commit to a thirty-minute conversation at least once a week in which you do not even mention the children. Regularly participate in activities that you will enjoy together long after the kids have gone out on their own.

LONG AFTER THE CHILDREN ARE GONE, YOU WILL STILL HAVE EACH OTHER.

48

ENCOURAGE GIGGLING.

*good laugh is sunshine in a house.*

Few people actually laugh themselves to death, but many do succumb to stress-related illnesses such as heart attacks and strokes. A healthy dose of humor can make a significant contribution to your overall health and well-being, including your marriage relationship.

Science is learning what common sense has shown us all along: Laughter is wonderful medicine and an important aid to healing. It revitalizes and relieves tension. No matter what problems you face today, look for humor and share a healthy chuckle or two with your mate.

FEW THINGS ARE MORE ENJOYABLE AND MEMORABLE THAN LAUGHING TOGETHER.

49

KEEP PRIVATE THINGS PRIVATE.

---

*Now it is required that those
who have been given
a trust must prove faithful.*

1 CORINTHIANS 4:2

Trust is a fragile thing—hesitantly gained, quickly lost. The personal revelations, insecurities, and innermost thoughts that you and your mate share within your marriage represent a sacred trust. The secrets divulged between husband and wife during intimate moments of communication must be guarded at all cost.

You hold within your grasp the ability to crush your spouse's spirit. By sharing a single one of these private disclosures, you weaken your mate's confidence in you. Protect this information with the impenetrability of an armored truck. Ask yourself before you speak, *Would my mate feel comfortable with my sharing this? Is it something I would say if my spouse were here with me?*

SECRETS BETWEEN HUSBAND AND WIFE ARE SACRED.

50

TAKE CARE OF YOUR APPEARANCE.

Personal appearance is looking the best you can for the money.

In all likelihood, before you were married you went to great lengths to make yourself look your very best to your future mate. You stood in front of the mirror combing and recombing your hair until it looked just right. You used large quantities of mouthwash and deodorant and liberally applied your favorite cologne. Often these efforts are ignored when your dating days come to an end.

The energies you applied to "catching" your spouse should not be abandoned now. Go to the trouble of making yourself look good. Shave or apply fresh makeup. Keep yourself presentable and do your best to remain as attractive as you were when you first fell in love.

HONOR YOUR MATE BY LOOKING YOUR BEST.

51

UNDERSTAND WHAT YOUR
SPOUSE DOES FOR A LIVING.

Every man's affairs,
however little,
are important to himself.

Chances are, you and your spouse lead double lives—a life at home with the family and a life at work apart from each other. Once you say good-bye to one another in the morning, even if one of you stays at home, the two of you head off to separate worlds. Each is filled with people and tasks that will continue to affect your moods and attitudes when you come back together in the evening.

For a full and healthy marriage, take time to understand and converse with each other about the daily challenges you face on the job. Accompany each other to company functions and meet coworkers with enthusiasm. Strive to know and understand the worlds you live in apart from one another.

YOUR WORK LIFE IS TOO IMPORTANT NOT TO SHARE.

52

REFUSE TO KEEP SCORE.

[Love] will hardly even
notice when
others do it wrong.

1 CORINTHIANS 13:5 TLB

Whether you have been married fifty years or five months, you and your spouse have a history. And, undoubtedly, somewhere in that history lurk instances of insensitivity on the part of your mate. Perhaps they spoke harsh words in an angry moment or acted less than loving at a time when you needed love the most.

Often, couples haul in the heavy artillery of past grievances when they enter a fresh battlefield. Such tactics only add fuel to the fight and never aid in the peacekeeping effort. So before your next conflict, make an agreement with your mate. Agree never to insert past issues into today's conflicts. Stay in the present tense when you face marital discord.

DON'T KEEP A LIST OF "WRONGS REMEMBERED."

53

VALUE YOUR SPOUSE'S OPINION.

We are of different opinions at different hours, but we always may be said to be at heart on the side of truth.

In those times when you search for wisdom, where are you likely to turn? A pastor? A psychologist? Both may be excellent options, so don't rule out either of these resources. However, before you go searching for a wise sage, seek the opinion of your spouse.

So often, we fail to appreciate fully those with whom we are most familiar. Their insight appears commonplace when we are around them constantly. What a shame! These are the very people who have a personal stake in our happiness and success. Don't foolishly disregard this important resource. Place a high value on your spouse's opinion.

THE BEST COUNSEL YOU EVER GET MAY COME FROM YOUR OWN HOME.

54

KEEP A JOURNAL OF YOUR
FAVORITE SHARED MEMORIES.

God gave us our memories
so that we might
have roses in December.

Certain moments should be cherished forever. Yet as time passes, our memories fade and fail. Think back. Can you still vividly recall how your spouse acted on that first date? Do you remember the soft, sweet words the two of you shared privately on the night before your wedding?

Years from now, the mere reading of a yellowed-with-age journal entry can transport you back in time to a special event. Moreover, when the going gets rough, a reminder of happier times may provide that extra "oomph" you need to succeed. Make your memories last a lifetime. Write them down.

MAINTAIN A WRITTEN RECORD OF YOUR MARRIAGE'S MEMORABLE MOMENTS.

55

ACCEPT YOUR SPOUSE
WITHOUT RESERVATION.

ccept one another, then, just as
Christ accepted you,
in order to bring praise to God.

ROMANS 15:7

Many people spend their entire lives searching for acceptance. Rejection by their parents may have a lot to do with their searching and constant attempts to measure up. A marriage is the one place where your spouse should expect to feel unconditionally loved.

Your spouse must not sense that you are always trying to mold them into your ideal perfect mate. Avoid comparisons. Accept your spouse without stipulations or demands. Grant permission for your spouse to be real, unfettered, and relaxed.

REAL LOVE ACCEPTS OTHERS
JUST AS THEY ARE.

56

APPRECIATE THE LITTLE THINGS
YOUR SPOUSE DOES.

---

*I*t has long been an axiom of mine
that the little things are
infinitely the most important.

Too often when two people live together for an extended period, they begin to take each other for granted. Little kindnesses have a way of becoming expectations. When these expectations aren't met, resentment can set in.

Practicing an attitude of gratefulness is a good way to keep a fresh appreciation for the little things your spouse does to care for you and your family. It serves as a reminder to say, "Thank you," and keeps your spouse feeling that their actions on your behalf are noticed. Gratefulness is a great boost to marital happiness.

A LITTLE APPRECIATION
GOES A LONG WAY.

57

DREAM BIG DREAMS
WITH YOUR SPOUSE.

"*No eye has seen, no ear has heard,
no mind has conceived
what God has prepared
for those who love him.*"

1 CORINTHIANS 2:9

Dreams of future possibilities inoculate us from despair. They remind us that no matter how depressing our present circumstance, potential exists for a brighter tomorrow. Dreams encourage our spirits and keep us looking up.

Shoot for the moon as you consider the direction you want your lives to take. Join with your mate in exploring a universe full of future destinations. Then live today expecting that someday your dreams will come true. The results may surprise you. Shared dreams lead to shared optimism, share opportunities, and most often, shared fulfillment.

TWO CAN DREAM BIGGER
AND ACCOMPLISH
MORE THAN ONE.

58

LEARN TO LAUGH AT YOURSELF.

e who has learned to laugh at
himself shall never
cease to be entertained.

When you're in a hurry, have you been known to make silly mistakes, such as spraying hair spray where the deodorant should go or vice versa? Look for the humor in your absentmindedness rather than grimacing in embarrassment. Have a healthy laugh at your own expense.

People who can laugh at themselves make better marriage partners. They tend to be more flexible, tolerant, and well-adjusted. Laughing at yourself keeps your ego in check and your feet on the ground. If you have never learned to laugh at yourself, now is a good time to do it. A strong marriage depends on it.

THAT PERSON YOU SEE IN THE MIRROR MAY BE YOUR BEST SOURCE FOR COMIC RELIEF.

59

TAKE OFF YOUR WATCH.

Hour by hour I place my days
in your hand.

PSALM 31:15 MSG

In a rush? Clock-watching can actually waste time and increase your anxiety. Sometimes you can't avoid it, but this weekend, try observing your inner clock rather than the watch on your wrist. Eat when you are hungry. Sleep when you are tired. Work or play when you are energized. Then, take what you've learned about your own daily rhythms and apply it to your regular schedule. It can help you get more done in less time. And with the reduced stress, you'll be a more pleasant person for your beloved.

Use the time that you are most alert to plan, organize, and tackle your toughest projects. If you fall into an afternoon slump, schedule tasks that don't take a lot of brainpower, like returning phone calls. And when your body says, "Time for bed," listen! It won't just help you—it will help keep your love alive.

UNDERSTANDING WHAT MAKES YOU TICK CAN HELP MAKE OTHER AREAS IN YOUR LIFE CLICK.

60

COMMEMORATE IMPORTANT DATES.

I've a grand memory
for forgetting.

Red-letter days such as Valentine's Day, birthdays, and anniversaries aren't likely to slip by unobserved. But if they do so regularly, it is more often the result of carelessness and insensitivity than forgetfulness.

Remembering those dates without being reminded will make a big impression on your spouse. Why? Because it indicates that you deeply value your relationship. It reaffirms your love and emphasizes your commitment to keep your marriage fresh and grounded in love. Don't treat these special occasions as just more dates to remember. Honor them as opportunities to celebrate your marriage and to keep your love alive.

MEMORIALIZE THE MILESTONES OF YOUR MARRIAGE.

61

FIGHT FAIR.

*ot tempers start fights;*
a calm, cool spirit

keeps the peace.

PROVERBS 15:18 MSG

Disagreements are inevitable in any marriage. Arguments occur between the most loving mates. In a moment when calm and reason prevail, make a pact always to play by the rules. Your mutually agreed-upon list of rules may read something like this:

- Neither party shall resort to or threaten violence in any form.

- Neither party shall run home to mother.

- Neither party shall sleep on the couch.

- Either party may request a brief cooling-off period to regain emotional control, but the time period should be measured in hours, not days or weeks.

Your list should be unique to the two of you, but once you make your list, play fair. Abide by the rules.

PLAYING BY THE RULES
WILL PRODUCE A
WINNING MARRIAGE.

62

MAKE A LIST OF THINGS YOU LOVE ABOUT YOUR SPOUSE.

*ow do I love thee?
Let me count the ways.*

You might as well face the facts. You won't necessarily feel attracted to your spouse when you gaze into their sleep-matted eyes in the morning. You may need an occasional reminder of what you ever found attractive in the first place.

Prepare now for the day when the mystique of marriage fades and the excitement melts into commonplace. Keep a record of all the reasons you fell in love with your mate. Add to your list regularly and freely share your insights. You are likely to find that your spouse rewards you by working hard to preserve those things you appreciate most.

USE YOUR WORDS TO REKINDLE YOUR LOVE.

63

PICK UP AFTER YOURSELF.

What separates two people most
profoundly is a different
sense and degree of cleanliness.

Are yesterday's clothes draped across the treadmill? Has the mail accumulated on the credenza so long that the pizza coupons have expired?

When frequently needed items aren't put away properly, chances are you'll spend countless minutes of your life frantically searching for them when you're ready to walk out the door. Even worse, if your spouse takes the responsibility of picking up after you, they may resent the implication that your time is intrinsically more valuable. Clean up your own clutter, and you're likely to find more minutes in your day—and a more cheerful spouse.

IF YOU USE IT,
PUT IT AWAY.

64

GUARD YOUR SPOUSE'S
NEED FOR REST.

*"Come to me and I will give you rest—
all of you who work so hard
beneath a heavy yoke."*

MATTHEW 11:28 TLB

A good nap is a treasure these days. If yard work and home maintenance don't interfere with our need for sleep, the kids or the telephone will. We cram so much into each day that we rarely find time to unwind. Adults still need to get proper rest. Without sufficient downtime, no one can function at peak capacity.

If you want to see true appreciation in your spouse's eyes, suggest that the two of you take a nap together. Resist the urge to fill every minute of your weekends with chores and errands. If you can't take a nap together, offer to keep things under control so your spouse can chill out for an hour or two. You'll be surprised as you see how many ways your kindness makes things better for everyone in the family.

THE WHOLE WORLD
LOOKS BRIGHTER
THROUGH RESTED EYES.

ALLOW YOUR SPOUSE THE
BENEFIT OF THE DOUBT.

At the gate which suspicion enters,
love goes out.

Jumping to conclusions can land a couple smack-dab in the middle of a sticky relational mess. Accusations and questions of loyalty can drive a deep wedge between mates, virtually halting communication.

Mistrust without cause often reveals your own insecurities and jealousies. But what are you to do when such feelings stab at your confidence in your mate? When you catch the first whispers of suspicion, discuss them with your mate immediately. Ask his or her advice on ways to deal with your uncomfortable feelings. Reinforce your trust while confessing your own insecurities. Focus on "me" and "I." Refrain from pointing the finger and leveling blame with an accusatory "you."

BEING ABLE TO TRUST ONE ANOTHER IS FOUNDATIONAL TO A HAPPY MARRIAGE.

66

SING IN THE CAR.

Music hath charms to soothe the savage beast.

Caught in rush hour? Drowning in the deep end of the car pool? Running the same old errands week after week? Instead of taking out your frustrations by telling others how to drive or taking it out on your spouse when you get home, give your vocal chords a harmonious workout. Turn on your favorite radio station. Put in a tape or CD that really gets your blood pumping. Then sing along. Croon. Warble. Worship. Hum. Use your steering wheel as a drum set.

And don't worry about what other drivers think. You'll probably make them smile. Before you know it, you'll arrive at your destination with a smile of your own.

EVEN IF YOU CAN'T CARRY A TUNE, A TUNE CAN HELP CARRY YOU.

67

REALIZE THAT PEOPLE
HAVE DIFFERENT WAYS
OF SHOWING LOVE.

*The heart has its reasons
which reason
knows nothing of.*

A pie made from scratch may be a wife's deepest expression of love, while a husband may show his love with gifts or verbal tokens of appreciation. If your way of showing love is vastly different from your mate's, consider the training ground of their childhood. How did your spouse's parents express love in the home? Did they openly show affection, or did they express their love in more subtle ways?

Our ways of expressing love are as different as our personalities. Our backgrounds influence our ability to convey the emotions of our hearts. Should you start to feel insecure about your spouse's love, consider the possibility that they are simply expressing devotion in ways unfamiliar to you.

UNDERSTANDING EACH
OTHER'S EXPRESSION OF
LOVE WILL INCREASE YOUR
APPRECIATION OF IT.

68

SHARE CHORES AND DO
MORE THAN YOUR SHARE.

---

wo can accomplish more than twice as much as one.

ECCLESIASTES 4:9 TLB

Life gets dirty. The management of a household, no matter how big or small, entails a never-ending cycle of chores. Sit down together and draw up a list of jobs for each of you. Some couples divvy up the workload by assigning one spouse all outdoor chores, while the other handles the work inside the four walls of the house. Others like to share chores inside the house and out. Determine what works best for you.

Don't become resentful when your spouse leaves something undone. Do the task cheerfully and don't make a big deal of it. Make a conscious effort to maintain a proper heart and attitude, serving each other lovingly.

SHARING CHORES IS A TANGIBLE WAY TO SHOW LOVE.

CHERISH THE EVERYDAY MOMENTS.

Cherish all your happy moments:
they make a fine cushion
for old age.

We bide our time between vacations and holidays, eager for the next special event on the calendar to roll around, when we should savor each moment of our time on Earth. The lion's share of life isn't composed of holidays and special occasions. We do most of our living in the ordinary, everyday here and now.

In the course of a long-term marriage, there are many special events. But more than anything else, there are the ordinary days that make up your life with your spouse. Don't wait for a special occasion to notice your spouse's smile or thank God for bringing you together. Enjoy each moment.

ENJOY EACH MOMENT
WITH YOUR MATE.
IT IS GOD'S GIFT TO YOU.

70

SPEND YOUR MONEY WISELY.

Beware of the little expenses.
A small leak will
sink a great ship.

A wealth of financial books abound, but the best advice regarding fiscal responsibility can be summed up in the following words:

- Don't let your outgo surpass your income.

- Save or invest 10 percent of your take-home pay.

- Before resorting to credit purchases, ask yourself if the item will outlive the debt.

- Live simply. Downsize if need be.

- Put God first with your finances. Give a tithe of 10 percent to your local church.

- Don't stretch your budget so thin that you can't assist those in need.

- Cling loosely to material things. Instead, invest your life in that which transcends earthly wealth.

KEEPING MONEY UNDER CONTROL HELPS KEEP A MARRIAGE STRONG.

71

BE NICE TO YOUR
SPOUSE'S COWORKERS.

o your part to live in peace
with everyone,
as much as possible.

ROMANS 12:18 TLB

You know that awful grouch your spouse works with—or for? The one who leaves your mate frustrated or irritated by the end of the day? Even if you never meet your spouse's coworkers face-to-face, you can play an important role in their workplace relationships.

Don't be quick to judge or criticize. Encourage your spouse to verbalize the positive characteristics of those they work with. Suggest ways to build bridges and mend fences. It is important to express empathy for your spouse's situation but resist the urge to reinforce hurt feelings by taking on your spouse's offense. Your lives will be happier and your marriage stronger when you make a habit of encouraging each other to do the right thing.

BE AN EXAMPLE TO ONE ANOTHER OF LOVE AND GOOD WORKS.

72

GIVE A SPECIAL GIFT—JUST TO SAY, "I LOVE YOU."

---

et him that desires to see others happy make haste to give while his gift can be enjoyed, and remember that every moment of delay takes away something from the value of his benefaction.

Be on the lookout wherever you go for fun trinkets and small gifts for your spouse. The presents need not be expensive purchases or time-consuming projects. Think in terms of items that will make your loved one smile. It can be something as simple as a magazine that you picked up while in the checkout line at the grocery store.

Focus your extravagance on the presentation—not the gift. Prepare some heartfelt words that express your deep sentiments. Let your spouse know you bought the gift simply as a reminder of your love. Little things can make a big difference in the life of your marriage.

GIFTS FROM THE HEART ARE PRICELESS—NO MATTER THE PURCHASE PRICE.

73

WILLINGLY SEEK OUTSIDE HELP
WHEN IT'S NEEDED.

*It can be no dishonor
to learn from others
when they speak good sense.*

There may come a day in your marriage when you and your mate reach an impasse. You feel like giving up. Your problems appear too big to solve, and you can't agree on anything. Before you throw in the towel, explore every available option for help.

Your marriage is the most precious human relationship you'll ever know. Preserve it no matter the cost. Unless you are in physical danger or your emotions are so volatile that you may cause harm to your spouse, commit to stick together and work things out. Enlist the aid of a pastor or a professional counselor as you work to mend your marriage and make it strong.

GOD CREATED MARRIAGE.
HE CAN HELP MEND YOURS.

74

CREATE A SAFE PLACE
TO SHARE IDEAS.

---

*An invasion of armies can
be resisted, but
not an idea whose time has come.*

Do you remember how it felt when you were a child and you drew a picture or made something and presented it to someone? Oftentimes as adults, we still have that heart-pounding experience when we share an idea with someone. Our minds warn us, *They may not like it!* But something in our spirits yearns to take a risk and share an idea. It's a matter of trust.

Maybe your spouse has an idea for a creative or meaningful get-together, an easier way to accomplish something, or a small-business idea. Make your mate feel safe by encouraging them to share ideas—half of the fun is in the talking and dreaming!

IDEAS CAN BE DIAMONDS
IN THE ROUGH.

75

SING YOUR SPOUSE'S PRAISES
IN FRONT OF YOUR CHILDREN.

What children hear at home soon flies abroad.

Children draw comfort from knowing their parents admire and respect one another. They feel secure when they see Mom and Dad grounded in their love. When you point out the good qualities of your spouse and expound on the reasons for your love, you give your children an increased sense of security. At the same time, you reinforce the standards you want your children to seek in a husband or wife. The ideals and expectations your children have for their future marriage partners are built upon what they see lived out by their parents each day.

Brag about your mate. Hold your spouse up as a model for your children. Reserve your gripes and complaints for your personal journal, and hold your tongue when you're tempted to criticize.

LIGHT THE WAY FOR FUTURE GENERATIONS— LET YOUR LOVE SHINE.

76

COOK TO PLEASE.

One cannot think well, love well, sleep well, if one has not dined well.

Express your love in edible ways by taking time to prepare your spouse's favorite foods. Cooking a great meal of special treats is a powerful reminder to your mate that you are thinking loving thoughts. Even if you have no culinary skill, you can brew the morning's first pot of coffee.

Plan time out of your busy schedule to prepare one of your spouse's favorite foods. Don't wait for the next special occasion. Add fresh meaning to the term "comfort food." If you don't happen to be a great cook, get creative. There are many ways to put a delicious meal on the table.

MEALS PRESENTED BY LOVING HANDS SATISFY MORE THAN HUNGER.

77

GIVE YOUR ANSWERING
MACHINE A WORKOUT.

---

*So much they talk'd,
so very little said.*

Home phone. Work phone. Cell phone. Pager. Some people can be reached anywhere at any time. Though it may be convenient, it can also become a time-wasting interruption and a source of stress.

Getting caller ID to screen unwanted calls is a small step toward independence. Then let your answering machine do its job on a more regular basis. Don't answer the phone during dinner or "family times." Use e-mail. At work, schedule a morning or two a week where it's common knowledge that others should "leave a message." Schedule time to return calls in the afternoon when your energy is not as high. Don't ignore those who call; just fit them into a more appropriate time slot.

TO PICK UP . . .
OR NOT TO PICK UP,
THAT IS THE QUESTION.

78

CELEBRATE YOUR DIFFERENCES.

*J will praise thee; for I am fearfully and
wonderfully made: marvellous are
thy works; and that my soul
knoweth right well.*

PSALM 139:14 KJV

God knew what He was doing when He made the first human prototypes. He made us male and female—different by decision and design. Our strengths and weaknesses dovetail through a divinely inspired plan. This is especially true in a strong marriage relationship.

When you are tempted to scratch your head in dismay and mumble, "Why does my mate act that way?" realize that God created the two of you to complement each other. Your differences add strength and uniqueness to your marriage. Capitalize on the opportunity to prove that the whole really is greater than the sum of its parts.

MARRIAGE IS AN OPPORTUNITY TO COMPLETE EACH OTHER.

79

WATCH YOUR WEIGHT.

*he one way to get thin*
is to reestablish
a purpose in life.

Our population is ever increasing in weight. Have you joined this growing crowd? Before you admit to dieting defeat and sink your teeth into another piece of chocolate cake, consider the negative impact your surplus weight may have on your marriage.

Excess weight robs your body of both mental and physical energy. Moreover, a poor self-image created by extra pounds can cause a loss of confidence and leave you feeling unattractive to your mate. That can't help but dampen your romantic interest. Excess weight can shorten your life and damage your health, putting your future lives together at risk. If you've tried without success, ask your doctor for help.

GETTING PROPER EXERCISE AND EATING A BALANCED DIET ARE SIGNS OF HONORING YOUR MATE.

80

HOLD YOUR SPOUSE'S FAMILY IN HIGH REGARD.

Nobody who has not been in the interior of a family can say what the difficulties of any individual of that family may be.

In-law jokes abound. But extended-family conflicts are no laughing matter. They quickly create stress and disharmony in marriage and can make life miserable. Often the problems we face with our in-laws could be avoided simply by showing them a little courtesy and a lot of respect.

In every conversation concerning your spouse's family, keep your comments positive. Leave the skeletons in the closet where they belong. Refrain from making your mate's mother the brunt of your jokes. Don't criticize Dad. Refuse to belittle or poke fun, no matter how unusual your mate's relatives seem to you. Remember that your spouse's family is now your family as well.

LOVING SOMEONE MEANS
LOVING WHOM THEY LOVE.

81

RESIST THE URGE TO NAG—ALWAYS.

 *nagging wife annoys like constant dripping.*

PROVERBS 19:13 TLB

Although women usually are blamed for nagging, men are often just as guilty. Nagging may be the single greatest contributor to that dreaded ailment, selective hearing. Before you accuse your spouse of never listening to you, ask yourself if you are guilty of nagging.

If your badgering produces a payoff now, beware. Even the most compliant mate will eventually tune out a demanding whine. Few people want to be known as a henpecked husband or a browbeaten wife. Harping and hounding seldom produce the desired result. Gently present your request. Say it once. Then wait. Allow plenty of time for your spouse to respond before approaching the subject again.

DESIGNATE YOUR HOME
AS A NO-NAG ZONE.

82

PLAN FOR TIME APART.

The best thinking has been done in solitude. The worst has been done in turmoil.

Regardless of the close relationship you share with your mate, there are times when you both need time alone. Human beings need personal space from time to time in order to grow and thrive. Solitude is necessary to secure peace of mind.

Set aside some time each week to process deep thoughts and to let your mind and imagination soar. Look at it as a private retreat to refresh your parched soul. If all else fails, lock yourself in the bathroom and soak in the tub for a while. Reconnect with your inner self. Urge your spouse to do the same. Those brief, quiet moments will do you both a world of good.

RETREAT. REFRESH.
REFUEL.

83

SAY YES MORE OFTEN.

---

ife is either a daring adventure

or nothing.

Complacency is detrimental to life and marriage, but with each passing year comes an ever-increasing opportunity to climb into a rut. We nestle ourselves into a comfortable routine and refuse to budge without putting up a fight.

Refuse to trudge methodically through another day with nothing of note to mark the passing of time. Set those fuddy-duddy ways aside and throw caution to the wind. Choose something daring for the two of you. Then talk it up to your spouse until they catch the vision. Behave unpredictably. Above all else, resist the temptation to conform to the mundane. Say yes to life and a more exciting marriage.

SEIZE THE DAY!
JUST SAY YES!

84

PRESENT A UNITED FRONT
IN PARENTING.

Unity makes strength, and since
we must be strong,
we must also be one.

"Mom would let me eat ice cream if she were here," the child pleaded. "No," came the father's firm reply. The child pulled out the heavy artillery by turning on the tears. At this, Dad delivered the classic response, "Stop that crying right now, or I'll give you something to cry about." The boy issued his final threat through pouting lips, "I'm gonna tell Mommy on you!"

If you are a parent, the moral of this story is obvious to you. Kids constantly work at evening the odds—and they sometimes outsmart us. Establish the ground rules for cooperative parenting long before your kids can talk. Stick together. Parenting issues can breach even the strongest marital relationship.

UNITED PARENTING RESULTS IN WELL-ADJUSTED KIDS AND STRONGER MARRIAGES.

85

DEVELOP YOUR OWN
SECRET LANGUAGE.

*The best of life is conversation,
and the greatest success
is confidence, or perfect understanding
between sincere people.*

Creating a secret language doesn't mean you have to study linguistics or enroll in a language institute. Undoubtedly, you and your spouse have already developed quite a vocabulary. Pause for a moment and think. When you are in a crowd, do you trade private glances that hold meaning to no one else? Do you have pet words that require your own secret code to decipher?

That unwritten dictionary shared only by the two of you provides a private means of communicating that no one else can translate. Silent signs such as a crinkled nose or a crooked grin exchanged at just the right moment serve to strengthen the bond of your relationship with your mate.

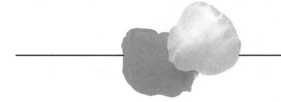

THE LANGUAGE OF LOVE NEEDS
LITTLE INTERPRETATION.

86

BREATHE IN, BREATHE OUT.

---

*The LORD God formed man of the
dust of the ground, and
breathed into his nostrils the breath
of life; and man became a living soul.*

GENESIS 2:7 KJV

Shallow breathing makes you feel tired. It lowers levels of oxygen and raises levels of carbon monoxide in your blood. It can also make your heart rate and blood pressure rise—adding stress on your body. And when you are uptight, it can create friction in the home.

When you feel tension mounting, try this deep-breathing exercise. Put your feet flat on the floor and rest your hands in your lap. Begin to relax your body by dropping your shoulders and closing your eyes. Then take a deep breath through your nose, while slowly counting to four. Exhale through your mouth to a slow count of four. Do this four times. You will feel your body relaxing, your fatigue lifting, and peace filling the atmosphere.

INSTEAD OF BEING UPTIGHT
AND OUT OF SIGHT,
BE A BREATH OF FRESH
AIR IN YOUR HOME.

87

SHOW RESPECT FOR YOUR PARENTS.

"*Honor your father and your mother,*
as the LORD your God
has commanded you."

DEUTERONOMY 5:16

We may adopt very different views than those of our parents. We may live vastly divergent lifestyles. Regardless of how much or little we feel we have in common with the people who raised us, we all retain several of our parents' characteristics. A part of them resides in us. When we respect our parents simply for who they are, we show respect for ourselves.

This attitude toward your parents sidetracks resentment and allows you to set legitimate, realistic boundaries for the relationship. Erratic, emotional reactions to parental expectations can be as stressful for your spouse as they are for you. Take the lead by determining to show respect for yourself and your parents.

YOU DON'T HAVE TO AGREE WITH YOUR PARENTS TO HONOR THEM.

88

NEVER TAKE YOUR SPOUSE
FOR GRANTED.

lways leave home with a tender good-bye and loving words. They may be the last.

Every day you live is a gift from God. Your home, spouse, children, job—even your life—are only on lease to you. You cannot know with certainty how long each lease will last. Therefore, if you have been blessed with another day, you have great reason to rejoice.

Anyone who has watched a spouse endure a life-threatening illness would tell you to celebrate daily the life of the one you love. Put aside petty disagreements. Let your spouse know how much you appreciate the blessing of sharing another day together. Life offers no guarantees; so don't take your life or your spouse's life for granted.

THANK GOD FOR YOUR
SPOUSE EVERY DAY.

89

GRANT YOUR SPOUSE SOME PRIVACY.

The human animal needs a freedom

seldom mentioned,

freedom from intrusion.

Not everything in marriage is community property. Grant one another some privacy. Don't resent or intrude on the need for personal space. If letters arrive addressed to your mate, resist the urge to open them. Impose a no-snooping rule. Don't eavesdrop on telephone conversations. Treat as sacred the secret contents of personal journals or diaries. That box of childhood memories and treasures should remain untouched until your mate is ready to share it with you.

When your spouse willingly reveals information, you will know that you have earned true trust—one of the most important elements of a strong marriage. Don't try to rush it. Build trust with time, and you'll discover it's well worth the effort.

A HAPPY MARRIAGE
INCLUDES RESPECT FOR
PERSONAL SPACE.

90

LEARN TO COMPROMISE.

You must get along with each other. You must learn to be considerate of one another, cultivating a life in common.

1 CORINTHIANS 1:10 MSG

No marriage can survive without some give-and-take from both parties. The literal meaning of the word *compromise* is "together to promise." You promise and give in just a bit. Don't always insist on having your every wish or demand fulfilled. If you give in occasionally, you will short-circuit a possible power struggle. You may find that you get your way more often when you let go of the need to win.

Your marriage vows are a commitment to reach a point of togetherness. This means giving, submitting, and letting go of your own demands. A great marriage brings together two independent and different individuals and makes them one. United in purpose, the spirits become intertwined so closely that they become one entity.

COMPROMISE MAKES IT EASIER FOR TWO PEOPLE TO BECOME ONE.

91

REMEMBER WHAT'S IMPORTANT.
FORGET WHAT'S NOT.

Now these three remain: faith, hope and love.
But the greatest of these is love.

1 CORINTHIANS 13:13

Many of us become stressed out over things that really won't matter when all is said and done. Step back long enough to evaluate your life priorities. Will the issues that eat at your thoughts today still matter a year—or five years—from now?

When we reach the end of life's journey, few of us will complain that we didn't accumulate more possessions. Neglected relationships and selfish attitudes could prove to be our deepest regrets. Prioritize the things that truly matter in life. Spend time nurturing family and friends. Give your marriage the attention it deserves. Reflect on your relationship with God. All of life's other urgencies take a backseat to these.

DON'T LET THE URGENT REPLACE THE IMPORTANT THINGS IN LIFE.

92

DO SOMETHING NICE FOR YOUR SPOUSE AND DO IT *FIRST*.

"*It is more blessed to give than to receive.*"

ACTS 20:35 TLB

Receiving is passive and an end in itself, but giving is active. It produces, generates, and creates. Those who give to others set into motion a cycle of blessing that often includes feelings of joy, happiness, satisfaction, fulfillment, and a deep, abiding sense of purpose. Nothing else in life produces so many benefits.

Giving *first* serves only to accentuate the experience. It is a genuine expression of love. Indeed, it is love's finest hour.

GIVING FIRST TO YOUR MATE IS ULTIMATELY THE BEST GIFT YOU CAN GIVE YOURSELF.

93

GET REGULAR PHYSICAL
AND DENTAL CHECKUPS.

*Life is not merely being alive
but being well.*

Medical and dental emergencies can be costly, time-consuming, and painful. Weigh the expense of such an incident against the time and money it takes to visit your doctor and dentist for regular checkups. You will find that prevention is a bargain.

However, the most important thing is to consider what your life would be like if you were to be stricken with a life-threatening illness or condition. Early detection can mean the difference between life and death. Do all you can while you can to keep your life unencumbered by the hardship of ill health. Your mate will appreciate it.

AN OUNCE OF PREVENTION
IS WORTH A POUND OF CURE.

94

PAY AS YOU GO.

Don't run up debts, except for the huge debt of love you owe each other.

ROMANS 13:8 MSG

Reader's Digest once reprinted an article from *Money* magazine entitled "Win Your War Against Debt." In the middle of the article, there was a two-page advertisement for a popular antidepressant! The irony of the placement of this ad may not have been intentional, but it conveyed a truth—debt can be depressing. Almost nothing zaps joy like a stack of unpaid bills marked "past due."

Some debt is unavoidable, but most indebtedness is self-inflicted. A "pay as you go" policy is the best way to get out of debt and stay out of debt. And the happiness of a debt-free life cannot be calculated.

HAPPINESS CANNOT
BE PURCHASED!

95

SEE THE WORLD—EVEN IF IT'S ONLY YOUR OWN NEIGHBORHOOD.

Voyage, travel, and change of place impart vigor.

Think for a moment about those places you and your mate would most like to see and map a plan to go there. Another state? Another nation? Why live like a hamster on a wheel, running in the same rut every day to the same places at the same times? Take time out! Establish a timetable for embarking on your personal adventure. The truth is, half the fun is the anticipation. So dream big and often!

In the meantime, take time out to discover the treasures in your own backyard and neighborhood. There's an amazing world within a few miles of you, waiting to be discovered and enjoyed.

HAPPINESS IS DISCOVERING THE WORLD AROUND YOU.

BE WILLING TO SHARE THE THINGS THAT MOVE YOU.

" *A man's heart determines his speech.* "

MATTHEW 12:34 TLB

In order to build intimacy in marriage, it's necessary to share things that touch your heart and affect you emotionally or spiritually. Don't take it for granted that your spouse knows all about you. If there's a song, quote, book, or movie that means a lot to you, share it. Then tell your spouse why it's significant to you and how it makes you feel or what it makes you think about.

Sharing the things that move you creates a point of bonding. It also helps you broaden your mate's perspective. If you hold back your thoughts, feelings, and opinions, there is little chance of deepening communication and learning what motivates and makes up the essence of your mate.

TO BE KNOWN TRULY,
WE MUST REVEAL TRULY.

97

BE QUICK TO ASK FOR FORGIVENESS.

"*Blessed are they whose transgressions are forgiven.*"

ROMANS 4:7

Forgiveness is a wonderful thing, and yet, much too often we allow our stubbornness to keep us burdened with guilt, struggling in our marriages, and feeling inadequate. The good news is that no one needs to live that way.

When we ask for forgiveness from God and those we have hurt or offended, we turn the tables on guilt and shame. A rush of joy, peace, and even elation soon follows. Why sit huddled in a dark corner of the doghouse when you can be running and playing in the sunshine of forgiveness? Remember that you also need to forgive yourself.

THE QUICKER YOU ASK FOR FORGIVENESS, THE SOONER YOUR MARRIAGE WILL BE BACK ON TRACK.

98

ATTEND MARRIAGE SEMINARS
AND RETREATS.

---

*How dear to this heart
are the scenes
of my childhood.*

Do you remember the carefree feeling you had as a child going off to summer camp? You can recapture that same sense of anticipation and fun as an adult and strengthen your marriage at the same time.

Marriage retreats and seminars provide a relaxed environment away from the routines and responsibilities of daily life. They're natural settings in which to spend time with your mate and focus on your relationship. And there's the added benefit of meeting other couples with whom you can get acquainted. With everyone hearing and reflecting on the same inspiring messages, meaningful conversation is sure to take place. Best of all, it's a time to reconnect with the one you love and fan the flames of intimacy and romance.

RETREAT TO GAIN IMPETUS TO MOVE FORWARD WITH YOUR MATE.

PINPOINT YOUR STRESSORS.

Know thyself.

Stress has earned a bad reputation. It's really a God-given response that triggers your body for fight or flight. It can spur you into action, saving your life in an emergency. But when feelings of stress linger or are triggered for little reason, they can deplete your body's resources. They can make you susceptible to heart disease, high blood pressure, even the common cold. You can become forgetful, disorganized, and less creative. Prolonged feelings of stress can also result in anxiety, aggression, or depression.

What are your biggest "stressors"? Procrastination? Perfectionism? Disorganization? A dead-end job? Illness? Unresolved conflict? Finances? Recognizing the main sources of stress for you and your mate is the first step toward reducing their effect on you. It will bring peace to your marriage and home.

IF YOU WANT "HOME, SWEET HOME," KICK STRESS OUT THE DOOR.

100

PUT THINGS BACK WHERE
YOU FOUND THEM.

---

*Be sure that everything is done
properly in a good
and orderly way.*

1 CORINTHIANS 14:40 TLB

The tape dispenser is missing in action. The cell phone is ringing, but not long enough to reveal its hiding place. You have to run a quick errand, but the car keys have disappeared. Your new camera goes on the fritz and the warranty is, well . . . you're sure you didn't throw it away!

How much time do you waste looking for something that should be right under your nose? How much extra stress is added to your day because you can't find what you need when you need it? Searching for lost items can be overwhelmingly stressful. Your mother was right: "A place for everything and everything in its place" is a simple principle that will bring peace and order to your home and relationship.

BEING ORGANIZED IN YOUR PERSONAL LIFE WILL HELP PRODUCE HARMONY IN THE HOME.

101

GIVE AND RECEIVE MORE HUGS.

*Love gives us in a moment what
we can hardly attain
by effort after years of toil.*

Hugs are powerful. They can take the hurt out of a child's scraped knee, heal a long-standing alienation, soothe a troubled soul, comfort the grieving heart, and put a smile on the face of almost any person who gives or receives one. Hugs are an expression of love without words. They speak for themselves, saying, "I care, I accept you, I value you, I've missed you, I like to be with you," and "I'm here for you."

Hugs are necessary for emotional growth. In fact, some researchers have concluded that children need as many hugs a day as they need glasses of milk. And marriage counselors often prescribe that spouses should hug at least twice a day. Don't forget to take your "hug for happiness" today!

HUMAN TOUCH CONNECTS YOU EMOTIONALLY AND PHYSICALLY TO EACH OTHER.

ACKNOWLEDGEMENTS

(8) Lynn Johnston, (12) Izaak Walton, (14) Abraham Lincoln, (20, 110, 174) Ralph Waldo Emerson, (22) O.A. Battista, (24) Martin Luther, (28) Emmanuel, (32) Katherine Mansfield, (34) Marcus Aurelius, (36) J.P. McEvoy, (38) W.H. Auden, (42, 134, 154) Thomas Fuller, (44) John Wanamaker, (46) Chinese Proverb, (50) William Somerset Maugham, (52) Thomas Moore, (56) Konrad Adenauer, (58) Charles Caleb Colton, (64) Aristotle, (66) Billy Graham, (68) Adlai Stevenson, (72, 120) John Powell, (76, 92) Mark Twain, (80) John Milton, (82) Franklin D. Roosevelt, (86) B.C. Forbes, (90) Charles Burton, (98) Robert Browning, (100) William Makepeace Thackeray, (104) Virginia Cary Hudson, (106, 148) Samuel Johnson, (112) Sir James Barrie, (116) Sir Arthur Conan Doyle, (124) Robert Louis Stevenson, (128) Elizabeth Barrett Browning, (130) Friedrich Nietzsche, (136) William Congreve, (138) Blaise Pascal, (142) Christopher Darlington Morley, (144) Benjamin Franklin, (150) Sophocles, (152) Victor Hugo, (156) Virginia Woolf, (158) Charles Churchill, (162) Cyril Connolly, (164) Jane Austen, (168) Thomas A. Edison, (170) Helen Keller, (172) Friedrich Von Baden, (180) Author Unknown, (182) Phyllis McGinley, (190) Martial, (194) Seneca, (200) Samuel Woodworth, (202) Plutarch, (206) Johann Wolfgang Von Goethe.

Additional copies of this book
are available from your local bookstore.

The following titles are also available
in this series:
101 Simple Secrets to Keep Your Faith Alive
101 Simple Secrets to Keep Your Hope Alive

If you have enjoyed this book,
or if it has impacted your life,
we would like to hear from you.
Please contact us at:
Honor Books
An Imprint of Cook Communications Ministries
4050 Lee Vance View
Colorado Springs, CO 80918
www.cookministries.com